SORT YOUR $HIT OUT

A MONTHLY BUDGET PLANNER

A Monthly Budget Planner: Sort Your $hit Out!
by Jackson A David

The font used on the copyright and disclaimer pages of this book is FreeSans. This font is licensed as GPL (GNU General Public License) which permits a font to be used on the cover and interior of a commercially available physical book.

The font used on the cover, the page titles, and for the date numbers on the tracking pages is Roboto (copyright Christian Robertson). The font used for the monthly tabs is Roboto Bold (copyright Christian Robertson). The Roboto family of fonts is available under the Apache License v2.00 which permits the font to be used on the cover and interior of a commercially available physical book.

The emoticon images used at the end of each month are derived from a single image (copyright kanate). This image was purchased from Adobe Stock with a Standard License, which permits the image to be used in a product for resale providing the main value of the product is not the image itself.

The images used on the monthly title pages throughout this book are derived from a single image (copyright hvostik16). This image was purchased from Adobe Stock with a Standard License, which permits the image to be used in a product for resale providing the main value of the product is not the image itself.

The handwriting font used throughout this book is Segoe Print. A Desktop License for this font was purchased from Fonts.com. A Desktop License permits the use of a font on the cover and interior of commercially available physical books.

The images of notepad pages used throughout this book are derived from a single image (copyright gmm2000) which was purchased from Adobe Stock with an Extended license. This license permits an image to be used on the cover and interior of a commercially available physical book where the image purchased forms a significant proportion of the value of the book.

ISBN: 9781678900540

You don't have to start this budget planner in January. If you start in a different month, then simply return to January at the end of the year to continue.

January

Create a Monthly Budget

****** MONEY COMING IN ******

Income 1	$
Income 2	$
Other income	$

TOTAL INCOME $ _____

****** MONEY GOING OUT ******

HOUSING

Mortgage or Rent	$
Real Estate Taxes	$
Maintenance/Repairs	$
Insurance	$

UTILITIES

Electricity	$
Water	$
Gas/Oil	$
Sewer	$
Trash	$
Cable/Satellite	$
Internet	$
Phone/Cell Phones	$

ANIMALS/PETS

Veterinary Costs	$
Food/Miscellaneous	$

FAMILY

Groceries	$
Child Care/Sitter	$
Toiletries	$
Hair Care	$
School/College Fees	$
School Supplies	$
Maintenance Payments	$
Subscriptions	$
Organizational Dues	$
Children's Allowances	$

HOUSEHOLD

Decorating/Furnishing	$
Garden	$
House Cleaning	$
Household Items	$
Laundry/Dry Cleaning	$

HEALTH

Life Insurance	$
Health Insurance	$
Dental Insurance	$
Doctor Visits	$
Dentist	$
Optometrist	$
Medicine	$

TRANSPORTATION
Car Payment/s $

Fuel $

Maintenance/Repair $

Insurance $

Travel Fares/Tickets $

CLOTHING
Adult/s $

Children $

CELEBRATIONS
Birthday/s $

Christmas/Holidays $

RECREATION
Entertainment $

Dining Out $

Socializing $

Vacation $

DEBTS
Credit Card #1 $

Credit Card #2 $

Credit Card #3 $

Credit Card #4 $

Other Debts $

SAVINGS
Emergency Fund $

Retirement Fund $

College Fund $

Pension Contributions $

OTHER OUTGOINGS
$

$

TOTAL OUTGOINGS $ _____

**** BUDGET CALCULATION ****

TOTAL INCOME $

– TOTAL OUTGOINGS $ _____

$ _____

If your total outgoings are greater than your total income, then you could find yourself getting further and further into debt. If this is the case, then it is important that you address the situation. You can do this by **REDUCING YOUR NON-ESSENTIAL SPENDING** and/or **INCREASING YOUR INCOME.**

Track Your Daily Spending

circle the day →

M T W Th F S Su	**1**st
Description	Amount

Daily Total:

M T W Th F S Su	**2**nd
Description	Amount

Daily Total:

M T W Th F S Su	**3**rd
Description	Amount

Daily Total:

M T W Th F S Su	**4**th
Description	Amount

Daily Total:

M T W Th F S Su — 5th

Description	Amount

Daily Total:

M T W Th F S Su — 6th

Description	Amount

Daily Total:

M T W Th F S Su — 7th

Description	Amount

Daily Total:

M T W Th F S Su — 8th

Description	Amount

Daily Total:

So far this month, I have spent: $

Track Your Daily Spending

circle the day

M T W Th F S Su   **9**th

Description	Amount

Daily Total:

M T W Th F S Su   **10**th

Description	Amount

Daily Total:

M T W Th F S Su   **11**th

Description	Amount

Daily Total:

M T W Th F S Su   **12**th

Description	Amount

Daily Total:

M T W Th F S Su 13th

Description	Amount
Daily Total:	

M T W Th F S Su 14th

Description	Amount
Daily Total:	

M T W Th F S Su 15th

Description	Amount
Daily Total:	

M T W Th F S Su 16th

Description	Amount
Daily Total:	

So far this month, I have spent: $

Track Your Daily Spending

circle the day →

M T W Th F S Su	**17**th
Description	Amount
Daily Total:	

M T W Th F S Su	**18**th
Description	Amount
Daily Total:	

M T W Th F S Su	**19**th
Description	Amount
Daily Total:	

M T W Th F S Su	**20**th
Description	Amount
Daily Total:	

M T W Th F S Su **21**st

Description	Amount

Daily Total:

M T W Th F S Su **22**nd

Description	Amount

Daily Total:

M T W Th F S Su **23**rd

Description	Amount

Daily Total:

M T W Th F S Su **24**th

Description	Amount

Daily Total:

So far this month, I have spent: **$**

Track Your Daily Spending

circle the day

M T W Th F S Su **25**th

Description	Amount
Daily Total:	

M T W Th F S Su **26**th

Description	Amount
Daily Total:	

M T W Th F S Su **27**th

Description	Amount
Daily Total:	

M T W Th F S Su **28**th

Description	Amount
Daily Total:	

M T W Th F S Su 29th

Description	Amount
Daily Total:	

M T W Th F S Su 30th

Description	Amount
Daily Total:	

M T W Th F S Su 31st

Description	Amount
Daily Total:	

** MONTHLY BUDGET CHECK **

MONTHLY INCOME $

- TOTAL SPEND $
_____

                      $
_____

How do you feel about your spending this month?

☹ ☹ 😐 🙂 😄

☐ ☐ ☐ ☐ ☐

I overspent   I was sensible!

What have you learned by tracking your spending this month? Write down your thoughts over the page.

WRITE DOWN YOUR THOUGHTS ABOUT THIS MONTH'S SPENDING

For example, you could ask yourself: Am I living within my means? Am I happier with my spending this month compared to last month? How can I cut down on non-essential spending? How can I increase my income? Can I afford a few treats? What lessons have I learned this month that I can put into practice next month?

February

Create a Monthly Budget

****** MONEY COMING IN ******

Income 1 $
Income 2 $
Other income $

TOTAL INCOME $ _____

****** MONEY GOING OUT ******

HOUSING

Mortgage or Rent $
Real Estate Taxes $
Maintenance/Repairs $
Insurance $

UTILITIES

Electricity $
Water $
Gas/Oil $
Sewer $
Trash $
Cable/Satellite $
Internet $
Phone/Cell Phones $

ANIMALS/PETS

Veterinary Costs $
Food/Miscellaneous $

FAMILY

Groceries $
Child Care/Sitter $
Toiletries $
Hair Care $
School/College Fees $
School Supplies $
Maintenance Payments $
Subscriptions $
Organizational Dues $
Children's Allowances $

HOUSEHOLD

Decorating/Furnishing $
Garden $
House Cleaning $
Household Items $
Laundry/Dry Cleaning $

HEALTH

Life Insurance $
Health Insurance $
Dental Insurance $
Doctor Visits $
Dentist $
Optometrist $
Medicine $

TRANSPORTATION
Car Payment/s	$
Fuel	$
Maintenance/Repair	$
Insurance	$
Travel Fares/Tickets	$

CLOTHING
Adult/s	$
Children	$

CELEBRATIONS
Birthday/s	$
Christmas/Holidays	$

RECREATION
Entertainment	$
Dining Out	$
Socializing	$
Vacation	$

DEBTS
Credit Card #1	$
Credit Card #2	$
Credit Card #3	$
Credit Card #4	$
Other Debts	$

SAVINGS
Emergency Fund	$
Retirement Fund	$
College Fund	$
Pension Contributions	$

OTHER OUTGOINGS
	$
	$

TOTAL OUTGOINGS $ _____

**** BUDGET CALCULATION ****

TOTAL INCOME	$
- TOTAL OUTGOINGS	$ _____
	$ _____

If your total outgoings are greater than your total income, then you could find yourself getting further and further into debt. If this is the case, then it is important that you address the situation. You can do this by **REDUCING YOUR NON-ESSENTIAL SPENDING** and/or **INCREASING YOUR INCOME.**

Track Your Daily Spending

circle the day →

| M T W Th F S Su | 1st |
Description	Amount
Daily Total:	

| M T W Th F S Su | 2nd |
Description	Amount
Daily Total:	

| M T W Th F S Su | 3rd |
Description	Amount
Daily Total:	

| M T W Th F S Su | 4th |
Description	Amount
Daily Total:	

M T W Th F S Su **5**th

Description	Amount

Daily Total:

M T W Th F S Su **6**th

Description	Amount

Daily Total:

M T W Th F S Su **7**th

Description	Amount

Daily Total:

M T W Th F S Su **8**th

Description	Amount

Daily Total:

So far this month, I have spent: **$**

Track Your Daily Spending

circle the day

M T W Th F S Su **9**th

Description	Amount

Daily Total:

M T W Th F S Su **10**th

Description	Amount

Daily Total:

M T W Th F S Su **11**th

Description	Amount

Daily Total:

M T W Th F S Su **12**th

Description	Amount

Daily Total:

M T W Th F S Su 13th

Description	Amount

Daily Total:

M T W Th F S Su 14th

Description	Amount

Daily Total:

M T W Th F S Su 15th

Description	Amount

Daily Total:

M T W Th F S Su 16th

Description	Amount

Daily Total:

So far this month, I have spent: $

Track Your Daily Spending

circle the day

M T W Th F S Su **17**th

Description	Amount

Daily Total:

M T W Th F S Su **18**

Description	Amount

Daily Total:

M T W Th F S Su **19**th

Description	Amount

Daily Total:

M T W Th F S Su **20**th

Description	Amount

Daily Total:

M T W Th F S Su 21st

Description	Amount
Daily Total:	

M T W Th F S Su 22nd

Description	Amount
Daily Total:	

M T W Th F S Su 23rd

Description	Amount
Daily Total:	

M T W Th F S Su 24th

Description	Amount
Daily Total:	

So far this month, I have spent: $

Track Your Daily Spending

circle the day

M T W Th F S Su **25**th

Description	Amount

Daily Total:

M T W Th F S Su **26**th

Description	Amount

Daily Total:

M T W Th F S Su **27**th

Description	Amount

Daily Total:

M T W Th F S Su **28**th

Description	Amount

Daily Total:

M T W Th F S Su 29th

Description	Amount

Daily Total:

← Only fill this in if it is a leap year.

** MONTHLY BUDGET CHECK **

MONTHLY INCOME $
− TOTAL SPEND $
$

How do you feel about your spending this month?

☹ ☹ 😐 😃 😄
☐ ☐ ☐ ☐ ☐
I overspent   I was sensible!

What have you learned by tracking your spending this month? Write down your thoughts over the page.

WRITE DOWN YOUR THOUGHTS ABOUT THIS MONTH'S SPENDING

For example, you could ask yourself: Am I living within my means? Am I happier with my spending this month compared to last month? How can I cut down on non-essential spending? How can I increase my income? Can I afford a few treats? What lessons have I learned this month that I can put into practice next month?

March

Create a Monthly Budget

****** MONEY COMING IN ******

Income 1	$
Income 2	$
Other income	$

TOTAL INCOME $ _____

****** MONEY GOING OUT ******

HOUSING

Mortgage or Rent	$
Real Estate Taxes	$
Maintenance/Repairs	$
Insurance	$

UTILITIES

Electricity	$
Water	$
Gas/Oil	$
Sewer	$
Trash	$
Cable/Satellite	$
Internet	$
Phone/Cell Phones	$

ANIMALS/PETS

Veterinary Costs	$
Food/Miscellaneous	$

FAMILY

Groceries	$
Child Care/Sitter	$
Toiletries	$
Hair Care	$
School/College Fees	$
School Supplies	$
Maintenance Payments	$
Subscriptions	$
Organizational Dues	$
Children's Allowances	$

HOUSEHOLD

Decorating/Furnishing	$
Garden	$
House Cleaning	$
Household Items	$
Laundry/Dry Cleaning	$

HEALTH

Life Insurance	$
Health Insurance	$
Dental Insurance	$
Doctor Visits	$
Dentist	$
Optometrist	$
Medicine	$

TRANSPORTATION
Car Payment/s $
Fuel $
Maintenance/Repair $
Insurance $
Travel Fares/Tickets $

CLOTHING
Adult/s $
Children $

CELEBRATIONS
Birthday/s $
Christmas/Holidays $

RECREATION
Entertainment $
Dining Out $
Socializing $
Vacation $

DEBTS
Credit Card #1 $
Credit Card #2 $
Credit Card #3 $
Credit Card #4 $
Other Debts $

SAVINGS
Emergency Fund $
Retirement Fund $
College Fund $
Pension Contributions $

OTHER OUTGOINGS
                         $
                         $

TOTAL OUTGOINGS $ _____

**** BUDGET CALCULATION ****

  TOTAL INCOME $
- TOTAL OUTGOINGS $ _____
                         $ _____

If your total outgoings are greater than your total income, then you could find yourself getting further and further into debt. If this is the case, then it is important that you address the situation. You can do this by **REDUCING YOUR NON-ESSENTIAL SPENDING** and/or **INCREASING YOUR INCOME.**

Track Your Daily Spending

circle the day

M T W Th F S Su　　1st

Description	Amount

Daily Total:

M T W Th F S Su　　2nd

Description	Amount

Daily Total:

M T W Th F S Su　　3rd

Description	Amount

Daily Total:

M T W Th F S Su　　4th

Description	Amount

Daily Total:

M T W Th F S Su — 5th

Description	Amount
Daily Total:	

M T W Th F S Su — 6th

Description	Amount
Daily Total:	

M T W Th F S Su — 7th

Description	Amount
Daily Total:	

M T W Th F S Su — 8th

Description	Amount
Daily Total:	

So far this month, I have spent: $

Track Your Daily Spending

circle the day

M T W Th F S Su	9th
Description	Amount
Daily Total:	

M T W Th F S Su	10th
Description	Amount
Daily Total:	

M T W Th F S Su	11th
Description	Amount
Daily Total:	

M T W Th F S Su	12th
Description	Amount
Daily Total:	

M T W Th F S Su 13th

Description	Amount
Daily Total:	

M T W Th F S Su 14th

Description	Amount
Daily Total:	

M T W Th F S Su 15th

Description	Amount
Daily Total:	

M T W Th F S Su 16th

Description	Amount
Daily Total:	

So far this month, I have spent: $

Track Your Daily Spending

circle the day

M T W Th F S Su   17th

Description	Amount

Daily Total:

M T W Th F S Su   18th

Description	Amount

Daily Total:

M T W Th F S Su   19th

Description	Amount

Daily Total:

M T W Th F S Su   20th

Description	Amount

Daily Total:

M T W Th F S Su 21st

Description	Amount

Daily Total:

M T W Th F S Su 22nd

Description	Amount

Daily Total:

M T W Th F S Su 23rd

Description	Amount

Daily Total:

M T W Th F S Su 24th

Description	Amount

Daily Total:

So far this month, I have spent: $

Track Your Daily Spending

circle the day

M T W Th F S Su **25**th

Description	Amount

Daily Total:

M T W Th F S Su **26**th

Description	Amount

Daily Total:

M T W Th F S Su **27**th

Description	Amount

Daily Total:

M T W Th F S Su **28**th

Description	Amount

Daily Total:

M T W Th F S Su 29th

Description	Amount

Daily Total:

M T W Th F S Su 30th

Description	Amount

Daily Total:

M T W Th F S Su 31st

Description	Amount

Daily Total:

** MONTHLY BUDGET CHECK **

MONTHLY INCOME $

− TOTAL SPEND $ _____

$ _____

How do you feel about your spending this month?

☹ 🙁 😐 🙂 😄

☐ ☐ ☐ ☐ ☐

I overspent   I was sensible!

What have you learned by tracking your spending this month? Write down your thoughts over the page.

WRITE DOWN YOUR THOUGHTS ABOUT THIS MONTH'S SPENDING

For example, you could ask yourself: Am I living within my means? Am I happier with my spending this month compared to last month? How can I cut down on non-essential spending? How can I increase my income? Can I afford a few treats? What lessons have I learned this month that I can put into practice next month?

April

Create a Monthly Budget

****** MONEY COMING IN ******

Income 1 $
Income 2 $
Other income $

TOTAL INCOME $ _____

****** MONEY GOING OUT ******

HOUSING

Mortgage or Rent $
Real Estate Taxes $
Maintenance/Repairs $
Insurance $

UTILITIES

Electricity $
Water $
Gas/Oil $
Sewer $
Trash $
Cable/Satellite $
Internet $
Phone/Cell Phones $

ANIMALS/PETS

Veterinary Costs $
Food/Miscellaneous $

FAMILY

Groceries $
Child Care/Sitter $
Toiletries $
Hair Care $
School/College Fees $
School Supplies $
Maintenance Payments $
Subscriptions $
Organizational Dues $
Children's Allowances $

HOUSEHOLD

Decorating/Furnishing $
Garden $
House Cleaning $
Household Items $
Laundry/Dry Cleaning $

HEALTH

Life Insurance $
Health Insurance $
Dental Insurance $
Doctor Visits $
Dentist $
Optometrist $
Medicine $

TRANSPORTATION
Car Payment/s $
Fuel $
Maintenance/Repair $
Insurance $
Travel Fares/Tickets $

CLOTHING
Adult/s $
Children $

CELEBRATIONS
Birthday/s $
Christmas/Holidays $

RECREATION
Entertainment $
Dining Out $
Socializing $
Vacation $

DEBTS
Credit Card #1 $
Credit Card #2 $
Credit Card #3 $
Credit Card #4 $
Other Debts $

SAVINGS
Emergency Fund $
Retirement Fund $
College Fund $
Pension Contributions $

OTHER OUTGOINGS
     $
     $

TOTAL OUTGOINGS $ _____

**** BUDGET CALCULATION ****

TOTAL INCOME $
− TOTAL OUTGOINGS $ _____
     $ _____

If your total outgoings are greater than your total income, then you could find yourself getting further and further into debt. If this is the case, then it is important that you address the situation. You can do this by **REDUCING YOUR NON-ESSENTIAL SPENDING** and/or **INCREASING YOUR INCOME.**

Track Your Daily Spending

circle the day →

M T W Th F S Su   1st

Description	Amount
Daily Total:	

M T W Th F S Su   2nd

Description	Amount
Daily Total:	

M T W Th F S Su   3rd

Description	Amount
Daily Total:	

M T W Th F S Su   4th

Description	Amount
Daily Total:	

M T W Th F S Su **5**th

Description	Amount

Daily Total:

M T W Th F S Su **6**th

Description	Amount

Daily Total:

M T W Th F S Su **7**th

Description	Amount

Daily Total:

M T W Th F S Su **8**th

Description	Amount

Daily Total:

So far this month, I have spent: **$**

Track Your Daily Spending

circle the day

M T W Th F S Su **9**th

Description	Amount

Daily Total:

M T W Th F S Su **10**th

Description	Amount

Daily Total:

M T W Th F S Su **11**th

Description	Amount

Daily Total:

M T W Th F S Su **12**th

Description	Amount

Daily Total:

M T W Th F S Su 13th

Description	Amount
Daily Total:	

M T W Th F S Su 14th

Description	Amount
Daily Total:	

M T W Th F S Su 15th

Description	Amount
Daily Total:	

M T W Th F S Su 16th

Description	Amount
Daily Total:	

So far this month, I have spent: $

Track Your Daily Spending

circle the day

M T W Th F S Su **17**th

Description	Amount

Daily Total:

M T W Th F S Su **18**th

Description	Amount

Daily Total:

M T W Th F S Su **19**th

Description	Amount

Daily Total:

M T W Th F S Su **20**th

Description	Amount

Daily Total:

M T W Th F S Su **21**st

Description	Amount

Daily Total:

M T W Th F S Su **22**nd

Description	Amount

Daily Total:

M T W Th F S Su **23**rd

Description	Amount

Daily Total:

M T W Th F S Su **24**th

Description	Amount

Daily Total:

So far this month, I have spent: **$**

Track Your Daily Spending

circle the day

M T W Th F S Su **25**th

Description	Amount
Daily Total:	

M T W Th F S Su **26**th

Description	Amount
Daily Total:	

M T W Th F S Su **27**th

Description	Amount
Daily Total:	

M T W Th F S Su **28**th

Description	Amount
Daily Total:	

M T W Th F S Su 29th

Description	Amount

Daily Total:

M T W Th F S Su 30th

Description	Amount

Daily Total:

** MONTHLY BUDGET CHECK **

MONTHLY INCOME $

- TOTAL SPEND $ _____

$ _____

How do you feel about your spending this month?

☹ 🙁 😐 🙂 😄

☐ ☐ ☐ ☐ ☐

I overspent   I was sensible!

What have you learned by tracking your spending this month? Write down your thoughts over the page.

WRITE DOWN YOUR THOUGHTS ABOUT THIS MONTH'S SPENDING

For example, you could ask yourself: Am I living within my means? Am I happier with my spending this month compared to last month? How can I cut down on non-essential spending? How can I increase my income? Can I afford a few treats? What lessons have I learned this month that I can put into practice next month?

May

Create a Monthly Budget

****** MONEY COMING IN ******

Income 1 $

Income 2 $

Other income $

TOTAL INCOME $ _____

****** MONEY GOING OUT ******

HOUSING

Mortgage or Rent $

Real Estate Taxes $

Maintenance/Repairs $

Insurance $

UTILITIES

Electricity $

Water $

Gas/Oil $

Sewer $

Trash $

Cable/Satellite $

Internet $

Phone/Cell Phones $

ANIMALS/PETS

Veterinary Costs $

Food/Miscellaneous $

FAMILY

Groceries $

Child Care/Sitter $

Toiletries $

Hair Care $

School/College Fees $

School Supplies $

Maintenance Payments $

Subscriptions $

Organizational Dues $

Children's Allowances $

HOUSEHOLD

Decorating/Furnishing $

Garden $

House Cleaning $

Household Items $

Laundry/Dry Cleaning $

HEALTH

Life Insurance $

Health Insurance $

Dental Insurance $

Doctor Visits $

Dentist $

Optometrist $

Medicine $

TRANSPORTATION

Car Payment/s	$
Fuel	$
Maintenance/Repair	$
Insurance	$
Travel Fares/Tickets	$

CLOTHING

| Adult/s | $ |
| Children | $ |

CELEBRATIONS

| Birthday/s | $ |
| Christmas/Holidays | $ |

RECREATION

Entertainment	$
Dining Out	$
Socializing	$
Vacation	$

DEBTS

Credit Card #1	$
Credit Card #2	$
Credit Card #3	$
Credit Card #4	$
Other Debts	$

SAVINGS

Emergency Fund	$
Retirement Fund	$
College Fund	$
Pension Contributions	$

OTHER OUTGOINGS

| | $ |
| | $ |

TOTAL OUTGOINGS $ _____

**** BUDGET CALCULATION ****

TOTAL INCOME	$
- TOTAL OUTGOINGS	$ _____
	$ _____

If your total outgoings are greater than your total income, then you could find yourself getting further and further into debt. If this is the case, then it is important that you address the situation. You can do this by **REDUCING YOUR NON-ESSENTIAL SPENDING** and/or **INCREASING YOUR INCOME.**

Track Your Daily Spending

circle the day →

M T W Th F S Su **1**st

Description	Amount

Daily Total:

M T W Th F S Su **2**nd

Description	Amount

Daily Total:

M T W Th F S Su **3**rd

Description	Amount

Daily Total:

M T W Th F S Su **4**th

Description	Amount

Daily Total:

M T W Th F S Su **5**th

Description	Amount

Daily Total:

M T W Th F S Su **6**th

Description	Amount

Daily Total:

M T W Th F S Su **7**th

Description	Amount

Daily Total:

M T W Th F S Su **8**th

Description	Amount

Daily Total:

So far this month, I have spent: $

Track Your Daily Spending

circle the day

M T W Th F S Su   9th

Description	Amount
Daily Total:	

M T W Th F S Su   10th

Description	Amount
Daily Total:	

M T W Th F S Su   11th

Description	Amount
Daily Total:	

M T W Th F S Su   12th

Description	Amount
Daily Total:	

M T W Th F S Su 13th

Description	Amount

Daily Total:

M T W Th F S Su 14th

Description	Amount

Daily Total:

M T W Th F S Su 15th

Description	Amount

Daily Total:

M T W Th F S Su 16th

Description	Amount

Daily Total:

So far this month, I have spent: $

Track Your Daily Spending

circle the day

M T W Th F S Su **17**th

Description	Amount
Daily Total:	

M T W Th F S Su **18**th

Description	Amount
Daily Total:	

M T W Th F S Su **19**th

Description	Amount
Daily Total:	

M T W Th F S Su **20**th

Description	Amount
Daily Total:	

M T W Th F S Su 21st

Description	Amount

Daily Total:

M T W Th F S Su 22nd

Description	Amount

Daily Total:

M T W Th F S Su 23rd

Description	Amount

Daily Total:

M T W Th F S Su 24th

Description	Amount

Daily Total:

So far this month, I have spent: $

Track Your Daily Spending

circle the day →

M T W Th F S Su **25**th

Description	Amount
Daily Total:	

M T W Th F S Su **26**th

Description	Amount
Daily Total:	

M T W Th F S Su **27**th

Description	Amount
Daily Total:	

M T W Th F S Su **28**th

Description	Amount
Daily Total:	

M T W Th F S Su 29th

Description	Amount
Daily Total:	

M T W Th F S Su 30th

Description	Amount
Daily Total:	

M T W Th F S Su 31st

Description	Amount
Daily Total:	

** MONTHLY BUDGET CHECK **

MONTHLY INCOME $

– TOTAL SPEND $ _____

                     $ _____

How do you feel about your spending this month?

☹ ☹ 😐 🙂 😄

☐ ☐ ☐ ☐ ☐

I overspent   I was sensible!

What have you learned by tracking your spending this month? Write down your thoughts over the page.

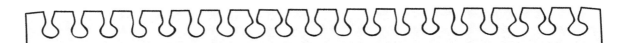

WRITE DOWN YOUR THOUGHTS ABOUT THIS MONTH'S SPENDING

For example, you could ask yourself: Am I living within my means? Am I happier with my spending this month compared to last month? How can I cut down on non-essential spending? How can I increase my income? Can I afford a few treats? What lessons have I learned this month that I can put into practice next month?

June

Create a Monthly Budget

****** MONEY COMING IN ******

Income 1 $

Income 2 $

Other income $

TOTAL INCOME $ _____

****** MONEY GOING OUT ******

HOUSING

Mortgage or Rent $

Real Estate Taxes $

Maintenance/Repairs $

Insurance $

UTILITIES

Electricity $

Water $

Gas/Oil $

Sewer $

Trash $

Cable/Satellite $

Internet $

Phone/Cell Phones $

ANIMALS/PETS

Veterinary Costs $

Food/Miscellaneous $

FAMILY

Groceries $

Child Care/Sitter $

Toiletries $

Hair Care $

School/College Fees $

School Supplies $

Maintenance Payments $

Subscriptions $

Organizational Dues $

Children's Allowances $

HOUSEHOLD

Decorating/Furnishing $

Garden $

House Cleaning $

Household Items $

Laundry/Dry Cleaning $

HEALTH

Life Insurance $

Health Insurance $

Dental Insurance $

Doctor Visits $

Dentist $

Optometrist $

Medicine $

TRANSPORTATION

Car Payment/s	$
Fuel	$
Maintenance/Repair	$
Insurance	$
Travel Fares/Tickets	$

CLOTHING

Adult/s	$
Children	$

CELEBRATIONS

Birthday/s	$
Christmas/Holidays	$

RECREATION

Entertainment	$
Dining Out	$
Socializing	$
Vacation	$

DEBTS

Credit Card #1	$
Credit Card #2	$
Credit Card #3	$
Credit Card #4	$
Other Debts	$

SAVINGS

Emergency Fund	$
Retirement Fund	$
College Fund	$
Pension Contributions	$

OTHER OUTGOINGS

	$
	$

TOTAL OUTGOINGS $ _____

_____

**** BUDGET CALCULATION ****

TOTAL INCOME	$
– TOTAL OUTGOINGS	$ _____
	$ _____

If your total outgoings are greater than your total income, then you could find yourself getting further and further into debt. If this is the case, then it is important that you address the situation. You can do this by **REDUCING YOUR NON-ESSENTIAL SPENDING** and/or **INCREASING YOUR INCOME.**

Track Your Daily Spending

circle the day →

M T W Th F S Su 1st

Description	Amount
Daily Total:	

M T W Th F S Su 2nd

Description	Amount
Daily Total:	

M T W Th F S Su 3rd

Description	Amount
Daily Total:	

M T W Th F S Su 4th

Description	Amount
Daily Total:	

M T W Th F S Su   **5**th

Description	Amount
Daily Total:	

M T W Th F S Su   **6**th

Description	Amount
Daily Total:	

M T W Th F S Su   **7**th

Description	Amount
Daily Total:	

M T W Th F S Su   **8**th

Description	Amount
Daily Total:	

So far this month, I have spent: **$**

Track Your Daily Spending

circle the day

M T W Th F S Su   **9**th

Description	Amount
Daily Total:	

M T W Th F S Su   **10**th

Description	Amount
Daily Total:	

M T W Th F S Su   **11**th

Description	Amount
Daily Total:	

M T W Th F S Su   **12**th

Description	Amount
Daily Total:	

M T W Th F S Su **13**th

Description	Amount

Daily Total:

M T W Th F S Su **14**th

Description	Amount

Daily Total:

M T W Th F S Su **15**th

Description	Amount

Daily Total:

M T W Th F S Su **16**th

Description	Amount

Daily Total:

So far this month, I have spent: $

Track Your Daily Spending

circle the day

M T W Th F S Su **17**th

Description	Amount

Daily Total:

M T W Th F S Su **18**th

Description	Amount

Daily Total:

M T W Th F S Su **19**th

Description	Amount

Daily Total:

M T W Th F S Su **20**th

Description	Amount

Daily Total:

M T W Th F S Su **21**st

Description	Amount

Daily Total:

M T W Th F S Su **22**nd

Description	Amount

Daily Total:

M T W Th F S Su **23**rd

Description	Amount

Daily Total:

M T W Th F S Su **24**th

Description	Amount

Daily Total:

So far this month, I have spent: $

Track Your Daily Spending

circle the day

M T W Th F S Su **25**th

Description	Amount
Daily Total:	

M T W Th F S Su **26**th

Description	Amount
Daily Total:	

M T W Th F S Su **27**th

Description	Amount
Daily Total:	

M T W Th F S Su **28**th

Description	Amount
Daily Total:	

M T W Th F S Su 29th

Description	Amount
Daily Total:	

M T W Th F S Su 30th

Description	Amount
Daily Total:	

** MONTHLY BUDGET CHECK **

MONTHLY INCOME $
- TOTAL SPEND $ _____
                     $ _____

How do you feel about your spending this month?

☹ ☹ 😐 😀 😄

☐ ☐ ☐ ☐ ☐

I overspent   I was sensible!

What have you learned by tracking your spending this month? Write down your thoughts over the page.

WRITE DOWN YOUR THOUGHTS ABOUT THIS MONTH'S SPENDING

For example, you could ask yourself: Am I living within my means? Am I happier with my spending this month compared to last month? How can I cut down on non-essential spending? How can I increase my income? Can I afford a few treats? What lessons have I learned this month that I can put into practice next month?

July

Create a Monthly Budget

****** MONEY COMING IN ******

Income 1	$
Income 2	$
Other income	$

TOTAL INCOME $ _____

****** MONEY GOING OUT ******

HOUSING

Mortgage or Rent	$
Real Estate Taxes	$
Maintenance/Repairs	$
Insurance	$

UTILITIES

Electricity	$
Water	$
Gas/Oil	$
Sewer	$
Trash	$
Cable/Satellite	$
Internet	$
Phone/Cell Phones	$

ANIMALS/PETS

Veterinary Costs	$
Food/Miscellaneous	$

FAMILY

Groceries	$
Child Care/Sitter	$
Toiletries	$
Hair Care	$
School/College Fees	$
School Supplies	$
Maintenance Payments	$
Subscriptions	$
Organizational Dues	$
Children's Allowances	$

HOUSEHOLD

Decorating/Furnishing	$
Garden	$
House Cleaning	$
Household Items	$
Laundry/Dry Cleaning	$

HEALTH

Life Insurance	$
Health Insurance	$
Dental Insurance	$
Doctor Visits	$
Dentist	$
Optometrist	$
Medicine	$

TRANSPORTATION

Car Payment/s $

Fuel $

Maintenance/Repair $

Insurance $

Travel Fares/Tickets $

CLOTHING

Adult/s $

Children $

CELEBRATIONS

Birthday/s $

Christmas/Holidays $

RECREATION

Entertainment $

Dining Out $

Socializing $

Vacation $

DEBTS

Credit Card #1 $

Credit Card #2 $

Credit Card #3 $

Credit Card #4 $

Other Debts $

SAVINGS

Emergency Fund $

Retirement Fund $

College Fund $

Pension Contributions $

OTHER OUTGOINGS

$

$

TOTAL OUTGOINGS $ _____

**** BUDGET CALCULATION ****

TOTAL INCOME $ _____

- TOTAL OUTGOINGS $ _____

$ _____

If your total outgoings are greater than your total income, then you could find yourself getting further and further into debt. If this is the case, then it is important that you address the situation. You can do this by **REDUCING YOUR NON-ESSENTIAL SPENDING** and/or **INCREASING YOUR INCOME.**

Track Your Daily Spending

circle the day

M T W Th F S Su — 1st

Description	Amount

Daily Total:

M T W Th F S Su — 2nd

Description	Amount

Daily Total:

M T W Th F S Su — 3rd

Description	Amount

Daily Total:

M T W Th F S Su — 4th

Description	Amount

Daily Total:

M T W Th F S Su   **5**th

Description	Amount
Daily Total:	

M T W Th F S Su   **6**th

Description	Amount
Daily Total:	

M T W Th F S Su   **7**th

Description	Amount
Daily Total:	

M T W Th F S Su   **8**th

Description	Amount
Daily Total:	

JUL

So far this month, I have spent: **$**

Track Your Daily Spending

circle the day →

M T W Th F S Su — 9th

Description	Amount
Daily Total:	

M T W Th F S Su — 10th

Description	Amount
Daily Total:	

M T W Th F S Su — 11th

Description	Amount
Daily Total:	

M T W Th F S Su — 12th

Description	Amount
Daily Total:	

M T W Th F S Su **13**th

Description	Amount
Daily Total:	

M T W Th F S Su **14**th

Description	Amount
Daily Total:	

M T W Th F S Su **15**th

Description	Amount
Daily Total:	

M T W Th F S Su **16**th

Description	Amount
Daily Total:	

So far this month, I have spent: **$**

Track Your Daily Spending

circle the day

M T W Th F S Su **17**th

Description	Amount

Daily Total:

M T W Th F S Su **18**th

Description	Amount

Daily Total:

M T W Th F S Su **19**th

Description	Amount

Daily Total:

M T W Th F S Su **20**th

Description	Amount

Daily Total:

M T W Th F S Su **21**st

Description	Amount

Daily Total:

M T W Th F S Su **22**nd

Description	Amount

Daily Total:

M T W Th F S Su **23**rd

Description	Amount

Daily Total:

M T W Th F S Su **24**th

Description	Amount

Daily Total:

So far this month, I have spent: **$**

Track Your Daily Spending

circle the day

M T W Th F S Su **25**th

Description	Amount

Daily Total:

M T W Th F S Su **26**th

Description	Amount

Daily Total:

M T W Th F S Su **27**th

Description	Amount

Daily Total:

M T W Th F S Su **28**th

Description	Amount

Daily Total:

M T W Th F S Su 29th

Description	Amount
Daily Total:	

M T W Th F S Su 30th

Description	Amount
Daily Total:	

M T W Th F S Su 31st

Description	Amount
Daily Total:	

** MONTHLY BUDGET CHECK **

MONTHLY INCOME $

− TOTAL SPEND $ _____

                  $ _____

How do you feel about your spending this month?

☹ 🙁 😐 🙂 😄

☐   ☐   ☐   ☐   ☐

I overspent   I was sensible!

What have you learned by tracking your spending this month? Write down your thoughts over the page.

WRITE DOWN YOUR THOUGHTS ABOUT THIS MONTH'S SPENDING

For example, you could ask yourself: Am I living within my means? Am I happier with my spending this month compared to last month? How can I cut down on non-essential spending? How can I increase my income? Can I afford a few treats? What lessons have I learned this month that I can put into practice next month?

August

AUG

Create a Monthly Budget

****** MONEY COMING IN ******

Income 1	$
Income 2	$
Other income	$

TOTAL INCOME $ _____

****** MONEY GOING OUT ******

HOUSING

Mortgage or Rent	$
Real Estate Taxes	$
Maintenance/Repairs	$
Insurance	$

UTILITIES

Electricity	$
Water	$
Gas/Oil	$
Sewer	$
Trash	$
Cable/Satellite	$
Internet	$
Phone/Cell Phones	$

ANIMALS/PETS

Veterinary Costs	$
Food/Miscellaneous	$

FAMILY

Groceries	$
Child Care/Sitter	$
Toiletries	$
Hair Care	$
School/College Fees	$
School Supplies	$
Maintenance Payments	$
Subscriptions	$
Organizational Dues	$
Children's Allowances	$

HOUSEHOLD

Decorating/Furnishing	$
Garden	$
House Cleaning	$
Household Items	$
Laundry/Dry Cleaning	$

HEALTH

Life Insurance	$
Health Insurance	$
Dental Insurance	$
Doctor Visits	$
Dentist	$
Optometrist	$
Medicine	$

TRANSPORTATION

Car Payment/s	$
Fuel	$
Maintenance/Repair	$
Insurance	$
Travel Fares/Tickets	$

CLOTHING

Adult/s	$
Children	$

CELEBRATIONS

Birthday/s	$
Christmas/Holidays	$

RECREATION

Entertainment	$
Dining Out	$
Socializing	$
Vacation	$

DEBTS

Credit Card #1	$
Credit Card #2	$
Credit Card #3	$
Credit Card #4	$
Other Debts	$

SAVINGS

Emergency Fund	$
Retirement Fund	$
College Fund	$
Pension Contributions	$

OTHER OUTGOINGS

	$
	$

TOTAL OUTGOINGS $ _____

**** BUDGET CALCULATION ****

TOTAL INCOME	$
- TOTAL OUTGOINGS	$ _____
	$ _____

If your total outgoings are greater than your total income, then you could find yourself getting further and further into debt. If this is the case, then it is important that you address the situation. You can do this by **REDUCING YOUR NON-ESSENTIAL SPENDING** and/or **INCREASING YOUR INCOME.**

Track Your Daily Spending

circle the day →

M T W Th F S Su   **1**st

Description	Amount

Daily Total:

M T W Th F S Su   **2**nd

Description	Amount

Daily Total:

M T W Th F S Su   **3**rd

Description	Amount

Daily Total:

M T W Th F S Su   **4**th

Description	Amount

Daily Total:

M T W Th F S Su **5**th

Description	Amount

Daily Total:

M T W Th F S Su **6**th

Description	Amount

Daily Total:

M T W Th F S Su **7**th

Description	Amount

Daily Total:

M T W Th F S Su **8**th

Description	Amount

Daily Total:

AUG

So far this month, I have spent: **$**

Track Your Daily Spending

circle the day

M T W Th F S Su **9**th

Description	Amount

Daily Total:

M T W Th F S Su **10**th

Description	Amount

Daily Total:

M T W Th F S Su **11**th

Description	Amount

Daily Total:

M T W Th F S Su **12**th

Description	Amount

Daily Total:

M T W Th F S Su **13**th

Description	Amount
Daily Total:	

M T W Th F S Su **14**th

Description	Amount
Daily Total:	

M T W Th F S Su **15**th

Description	Amount
Daily Total:	

M T W Th F S Su **16**th

Description	Amount
Daily Total:	

So far this month, I have spent: **$**

Track Your Daily Spending

circle the day

→ M T W Th F S Su **17**th

Description	Amount

Daily Total:

M T W Th F S Su **18**th

Description	Amount

Daily Total:

M T W Th F S Su **19**th

Description	Amount

Daily Total:

M T W Th F S Su **20**th

Description	Amount

Daily Total:

M T W Th F S Su **21**st

Description	Amount

Daily Total:

M T W Th F S Su **22**nd

Description	Amount

Daily Total:

M T W Th F S Su **23**rd

Description	Amount

Daily Total:

M T W Th F S Su **24**th

Description	Amount

Daily Total:

So far this month, I have spent: **$**

AUG

Track Your Daily Spending

circle the day

M T W Th F S Su **25**th

Description	Amount
Daily Total:	

M T W Th F S Su **26**th

Description	Amount
Daily Total:	

M T W Th F S Su **27**th

Description	Amount
Daily Total:	

M T W Th F S Su **28**th

Description	Amount
Daily Total:	

M T W Th F S Su 29th

Description	Amount

Daily Total:

M T W Th F S Su 30th

Description	Amount

Daily Total:

M T W Th F S Su 31st

Description	Amount

Daily Total:

** MONTHLY BUDGET CHECK **

MONTHLY INCOME $

- TOTAL SPEND $

$

How do you feel about your spending this month?

☹ ☹ 😐 😃 😄

☐ ☐ ☐ ☐ ☐

I overspent   I was sensible!

AUG

What have you learned by tracking your spending this month? Write down your thoughts over the page.

WRITE DOWN YOUR THOUGHTS ABOUT THIS MONTH'S SPENDING

For example, you could ask yourself: Am I living within my means? Am I happier with my spending this month compared to last month? How can I cut down on non-essential spending? How can I increase my income? Can I afford a few treats? What lessons have I learned this month that I can put into practice next month?

September

MONEY

SEP

Create a Monthly Budget

****** MONEY COMING IN ******

Income 1	$
Income 2	$
Other income	$

TOTAL INCOME $ _____

****** MONEY GOING OUT ******

HOUSING

Mortgage or Rent	$
Real Estate Taxes	$
Maintenance/Repairs	$
Insurance	$

UTILITIES

Electricity	$
Water	$
Gas/Oil	$
Sewer	$
Trash	$
Cable/Satellite	$
Internet	$
Phone/Cell Phones	$

ANIMALS/PETS

Veterinary Costs	$
Food/Miscellaneous	$

FAMILY

Groceries	$
Child Care/Sitter	$
Toiletries	$
Hair Care	$
School/College Fees	$
School Supplies	$
Maintenance Payments	$
Subscriptions	$
Organizational Dues	$
Children's Allowances	$

HOUSEHOLD

Decorating/Furnishing	$
Garden	$
House Cleaning	$
Household Items	$
Laundry/Dry Cleaning	$

HEALTH

Life Insurance	$
Health Insurance	$
Dental Insurance	$
Doctor Visits	$
Dentist	$
Optometrist	$
Medicine	$

TRANSPORTATION

Car Payment/s	$
Fuel	$
Maintenance/Repair	$
Insurance	$
Travel Fares/Tickets	$

CLOTHING

Adult/s	$
Children	$

CELEBRATIONS

Birthday/s	$
Christmas/Holidays	$

RECREATION

Entertainment	$
Dining Out	$
Socializing	$
Vacation	$

DEBTS

Credit Card #1	$
Credit Card #2	$
Credit Card #3	$
Credit Card #4	$
Other Debts	$

SAVINGS

Emergency Fund	$
Retirement Fund	$
College Fund	$
Pension Contributions	$

OTHER OUTGOINGS

	$
	$

TOTAL OUTGOINGS $ _____

**** BUDGET CALCULATION ****

TOTAL INCOME $ _____
- TOTAL OUTGOINGS $ _____
$ _____

If your total outgoings are greater than your total income, then you could find yourself getting further and further into debt. If this is the case, then it is important that you address the situation. You can do this by **REDUCING YOUR NON-ESSENTIAL SPENDING** and/or **INCREASING YOUR INCOME.**

Track Your Daily Spending

circle the day →

| M T W Th F S Su | 1st |
Description	Amount
Daily Total:	

| M T W Th F S Su | 2nd |
Description	Amount
Daily Total:	

| M T W Th F S Su | 3rd |
Description	Amount
Daily Total:	

| M T W Th F S Su | 4th |
Description	Amount
Daily Total:	

M T W Th F S Su — 5th

Description	Amount
Daily Total:	

M T W Th F S Su — 6th

Description	Amount
Daily Total:	

M T W Th F S Su — 7th

Description	Amount
Daily Total:	

M T W Th F S Su — 8th

Description	Amount
Daily Total:	

SEP

So far this month, I have spent: $

Track Your Daily Spending

circle the day

M T W Th F S Su **9**th

Description	Amount
Daily Total:	

M T W Th F S Su **10**th

Description	Amount
Daily Total:	

M T W Th F S Su **11**th

Description	Amount
Daily Total:	

M T W Th F S Su **12**th

Description	Amount
Daily Total:	

M T W Th F S Su **13**th

Description	Amount
Daily Total:	

M T W Th F S Su **14**th

Description	Amount
Daily Total:	

M T W Th F S Su **15**th

Description	Amount
Daily Total:	

M T W Th F S Su **16**th

Description	Amount
Daily Total:	

So far this month, I have spent: $

Track Your Daily Spending

circle the day

M T W Th F S Su **17**th

Description	Amount
Daily Total:	

M T W Th F S Su **18**th

Description	Amount
Daily Total:	

M T W Th F S Su **19**th

Description	Amount
Daily Total:	

M T W Th F S Su **20**th

Description	Amount
Daily Total:	

M T W Th F S Su **21**st

Description	Amount
Daily Total:	

M T W Th F S Su **22**nd

Description	Amount
Daily Total:	

M T W Th F S Su **23**rd

Description	Amount
Daily Total:	

M T W Th F S Su **24**th

Description	Amount
Daily Total:	

SEP

So far this month, I have spent: **$**

Track Your Daily Spending

circle the day

M T W Th F S Su **25**th

Description	Amount

Daily Total:

M T W Th F S Su **26**th

Description	Amount

Daily Total:

M T W Th F S Su **27**th

Description	Amount

Daily Total:

M T W Th F S Su **28**th

Description	Amount

Daily Total:

M T W Th F S Su 29th

Description	Amount
Daily Total:	

M T W Th F S Su 30th

Description	Amount
Daily Total:	

** MONTHLY BUDGET CHECK **

MONTHLY INCOME $

– TOTAL SPEND $ _____

                     $ _____

How do you feel about your spending this month?

☹ ☹ 😐 😃 😄

☐ ☐ ☐ ☐ ☐

I overspent   I was sensible!

What have you learned by tracking your spending this month? Write down your thoughts over the page.

WRITE DOWN YOUR THOUGHTS ABOUT THIS MONTH'S SPENDING

For example, you could ask yourself: Am I living within my means? Am I happier with my spending this month compared to last month? How can I cut down on non-essential spending? How can I increase my income? Can I afford a few treats? What lessons have I learned this month that I can put into practice next month?

October

OCT

Create a Monthly Budget

****** MONEY COMING IN ******

Income 1 $

Income 2 $

Other income $

_____

TOTAL INCOME $ _____

****** MONEY GOING OUT ******

HOUSING

Mortgage or Rent $

Real Estate Taxes $

Maintenance/Repairs $

Insurance $

UTILITIES

Electricity $

Water $

Gas/Oil $

Sewer $

Trash $

Cable/Satellite $

Internet $

Phone/Cell Phones $

ANIMALS/PETS

Veterinary Costs $

Food/Miscellaneous $

FAMILY

Groceries $

Child Care/Sitter $

Toiletries $

Hair Care $

School/College Fees $

School Supplies $

Maintenance Payments $

Subscriptions $

Organizational Dues $

Children's Allowances $

HOUSEHOLD

Decorating/Furnishing $

Garden $

House Cleaning $

Household Items $

Laundry/Dry Cleaning $

HEALTH

Life Insurance $

Health Insurance $

Dental Insurance $

Doctor Visits $

Dentist $

Optometrist $

Medicine $

TRANSPORTATION

Car Payment/s	$
Fuel	$
Maintenance/Repair	$
Insurance	$
Travel Fares/Tickets	$

CLOTHING

Adult/s	$
Children	$

CELEBRATIONS

Birthday/s	$
Christmas/Holidays	$

RECREATION

Entertainment	$
Dining Out	$
Socializing	$
Vacation	$

DEBTS

Credit Card #1	$
Credit Card #2	$
Credit Card #3	$
Credit Card #4	$
Other Debts	$

SAVINGS

Emergency Fund	$
Retirement Fund	$
College Fund	$
Pension Contributions	$

OTHER OUTGOINGS

	$
	$
TOTAL OUTGOINGS	$ _____

**** BUDGET CALCULATION ****

TOTAL INCOME	$
- TOTAL OUTGOINGS	$ _____
	$ _____

If your total outgoings are greater than your total income, then you could find yourself getting further and further into debt. If this is the case, then it is important that you address the situation. You can do this by **REDUCING YOUR NON-ESSENTIAL SPENDING** and/or **INCREASING YOUR INCOME.**

Track Your Daily Spending

circle the day →

M T W Th F S Su **1**st

Description	Amount

Daily Total:

M T W Th F S Su **2**nd

Description	Amount

Daily Total:

M T W Th F S Su **3**rd

Description	Amount

Daily Total:

M T W Th F S Su **4**th

Description	Amount

Daily Total:

| M T W Th F S Su | 5th |
Description	Amount
Daily Total:	

| M T W Th F S Su | 6th |
Description	Amount
Daily Total:	

| M T W Th F S Su | 7th |
Description	Amount
Daily Total:	

| M T W Th F S Su | 8th |
Description	Amount
Daily Total:	

OCT

So far this month, I have spent: $

Track Your Daily Spending

circle the day

M T W Th F S Su **9**th

Description	Amount

Daily Total:

M T W Th F S Su **10**th

Description	Amount

Daily Total:

M T W Th F S Su **11**th

Description	Amount

Daily Total:

M T W Th F S Su **12**th

Description	Amount

Daily Total:

M T W Th F S Su	13th
Description	Amount
Daily Total:	

M T W Th F S Su	14th
Description	Amount
Daily Total:	

M T W Th F S Su	15th
Description	Amount
Daily Total:	

M T W Th F S Su	16th
Description	Amount
Daily Total:	

So far this month, I have spent: $

Track Your Daily Spending

circle the day

M T W Th F S Su **17**th

Description	Amount

Daily Total:

M T W Th F S Su **18**th

Description	Amount

Daily Total:

M T W Th F S Su **19**th

Description	Amount

Daily Total:

M T W Th F S Su **20**th

Description	Amount

Daily Total:

M T W Th F S Su **21**st

Description	Amount

Daily Total:

M T W Th F S Su **22**nd

Description	Amount

Daily Total:

M T W Th F S Su **23**rd

Description	Amount

Daily Total:

M T W Th F S Su **24**th

Description	Amount

Daily Total:

OCT

So far this month, I have spent: **$**

Track Your Daily Spending

circle the day

M T W Th F S Su **25**th

Description	Amount

Daily Total:

M T W Th F S Su **26**th

Description	Amount

Daily Total:

M T W Th F S Su **27**th

Description	Amount

Daily Total:

M T W Th F S Su **28**th

Description	Amount

Daily Total:

M T W Th F S Su 29th

Description	Amount

Daily Total:

M T W Th F S Su 30th

Description	Amount

Daily Total:

M T W Th F S Su 31st

Description	Amount

Daily Total:

** MONTHLY BUDGET CHECK **

MONTHLY INCOME $

– TOTAL SPEND $ _____

$ _____

How do you feel about your spending this month?

☐ ☐ ☐ ☐ ☐

I overspent   I was sensible!

What have you learned by tracking your spending this month? Write down your thoughts over the page.

WRITE DOWN YOUR THOUGHTS ABOUT THIS MONTH'S SPENDING

For example, you could ask yourself: Am I living within my means? Am I happier with my spending this month compared to last month? How can I cut down on non-essential spending? How can I increase my income? Can I afford a few treats? What lessons have I learned this month that I can put into practice next month?

November

Create a Monthly Budget

****** MONEY COMING IN ******

Income 1	$
Income 2	$
Other income	$

TOTAL INCOME $ _____

****** MONEY GOING OUT ******

HOUSING

Mortgage or Rent	$
Real Estate Taxes	$
Maintenance/Repairs	$
Insurance	$

UTILITIES

Electricity	$
Water	$
Gas/Oil	$
Sewer	$
Trash	$
Cable/Satellite	$
Internet	$
Phone/Cell Phones	$

ANIMALS/PETS

Veterinary Costs	$
Food/Miscellaneous	$

FAMILY

Groceries	$
Child Care/Sitter	$
Toiletries	$
Hair Care	$
School/College Fees	$
School Supplies	$
Maintenance Payments	$
Subscriptions	$
Organizational Dues	$
Children's Allowances	$

HOUSEHOLD

Decorating/Furnishing	$
Garden	$
House Cleaning	$
Household Items	$
Laundry/Dry Cleaning	$

HEALTH

Life Insurance	$
Health Insurance	$
Dental Insurance	$
Doctor Visits	$
Dentist	$
Optometrist	$
Medicine	$

TRANSPORTATION
Car Payment/s $
Fuel $
Maintenance/Repair $
Insurance $
Travel Fares/Tickets $

CLOTHING
Adult/s $
Children $

CELEBRATIONS
Birthday/s $
Christmas/Holidays $

RECREATION
Entertainment $
Dining Out $
Socializing $
Vacation $

DEBTS
Credit Card #1 $
Credit Card #2 $
Credit Card #3 $
Credit Card #4 $
Other Debts $

SAVINGS
Emergency Fund $
Retirement Fund $
College Fund $
Pension Contributions $

OTHER OUTGOINGS
$
$

TOTAL OUTGOINGS $ _____

**** BUDGET CALCULATION ****

TOTAL INCOME $
- TOTAL OUTGOINGS $ _____
$ _____

If your total outgoings are greater than your total income, then you could find yourself getting further and further into debt. If this is the case, then it is important that you address the situation. You can do this by **REDUCING YOUR NON-ESSENTIAL SPENDING** and/or **INCREASING YOUR INCOME.**

Track Your Daily Spending

circle the day

M T W Th F S Su   1st

Description	Amount
Daily Total:	

M T W Th F S Su   2nd

Description	Amount
Daily Total:	

M T W Th F S Su   3rd

Description	Amount
Daily Total:	

M T W Th F S Su   4th

Description	Amount
Daily Total:	

M T W Th F S Su **5**th

Description	Amount

Daily Total:

M T W Th F S Su **6**th

Description	Amount

Daily Total:

M T W Th F S Su **7**th

Description	Amount

Daily Total:

M T W Th F S Su **8**th

Description	Amount

Daily Total:

NOV

So far this month, I have spent: **$**

Track Your Daily Spending

circle the day →

M T W Th F S Su	9th
Description	Amount
	Daily Total:

M T W Th F S Su	10th
Description	Amount
	Daily Total:

M T W Th F S Su	11th
Description	Amount
	Daily Total:

M T W Th F S Su	12th
Description	Amount
	Daily Total:

M T W Th F S Su **13**th

Description	Amount

Daily Total:

M T W Th F S Su **14**th

Description	Amount

Daily Total:

M T W Th F S Su **15**th

Description	Amount

Daily Total:

M T W Th F S Su **16**th

Description	Amount

Daily Total:

NOV

So far this month, I have spent: $

Track Your Daily Spending

circle the day →

M T W Th F S Su 17ᵗʰ

Description	Amount

Daily Total:

M T W Th F S Su 18ᵗʰ

Description	Amount

Daily Total:

M T W Th F S Su 19ᵗʰ

Description	Amount

Daily Total:

M T W Th F S Su 20ᵗʰ

Description	Amount

Daily Total:

M T W Th F S Su 21st

Description	Amount
Daily Total:	

M T W Th F S Su 22nd

Description	Amount
Daily Total:	

M T W Th F S Su 23rd

Description	Amount
Daily Total:	

M T W Th F S Su 24th

Description	Amount
Daily Total:	

So far this month, I have spent: $

Track Your Daily Spending

circle the day

M T W Th F S Su **25**th

Description	Amount

Daily Total:

M T W Th F S Su **26**th

Description	Amount

Daily Total:

M T W Th F S Su **27**th

Description	Amount

Daily Total:

M T W Th F S Su **28**th

Description	Amount

Daily Total:

M T W Th F S Su 29th

Description	Amount

Daily Total:

M T W Th F S Su 30th

Description	Amount

Daily Total:

** MONTHLY BUDGET CHECK **

MONTHLY INCOME $

– TOTAL SPEND $ _____

$ _____

How do you feel about your spending this month?

☐ ☐ ☐ ☐ ☐

I overspent   I was sensible!

What have you learned by tracking your spending this month? Write down your thoughts over the page.

WRITE DOWN YOUR THOUGHTS ABOUT THIS MONTH'S SPENDING

For example, you could ask yourself: Am I living within my means? Am I happier with my spending this month compared to last month? How can I cut down on non-essential spending? How can I increase my income? Can I afford a few treats? What lessons have I learned this month that I can put into practice next month?

December

Create a Monthly Budget

****** **MONEY COMING IN** ******

Income 1 $
Income 2 $
Other income $

TOTAL INCOME $ _____

****** **MONEY GOING OUT** ******

HOUSING

Mortgage or Rent $
Real Estate Taxes $
Maintenance/Repairs $
Insurance $

UTILITIES

Electricity $
Water $
Gas/Oil $
Sewer $
Trash $
Cable/Satellite $
Internet $
Phone/Cell Phones $

ANIMALS/PETS

Veterinary Costs $
Food/Miscellaneous $

FAMILY

Groceries $
Child Care/Sitter $
Toiletries $
Hair Care $
School/College Fees $
School Supplies $
Maintenance Payments $
Subscriptions $
Organizational Dues $
Children's Allowances $

HOUSEHOLD

Decorating/Furnishing $
Garden $
House Cleaning $
Household Items $
Laundry/Dry Cleaning $

HEALTH

Life Insurance $
Health Insurance $
Dental Insurance $
Doctor Visits $
Dentist $
Optometrist $
Medicine $

TRANSPORTATION
Car Payment/s $
Fuel $
Maintenance/Repair $
Insurance $
Travel Fares/Tickets $

CLOTHING
Adult/s $
Children $

CELEBRATIONS
Birthday/s $
Christmas/Holidays $

RECREATION
Entertainment $
Dining Out $
Socializing $
Vacation $

DEBTS
Credit Card #1 $
Credit Card #2 $
Credit Card #3 $
Credit Card #4 $
Other Debts $

SAVINGS
Emergency Fund $
Retirement Fund $
College Fund $
Pension Contributions $

OTHER OUTGOINGS
    $
    $

TOTAL OUTGOINGS $ _____

**** BUDGET CALCULATION ****

    TOTAL INCOME $
    - TOTAL OUTGOINGS $ _____
    $ _____

If your total outgoings are greater than your total income, then you could find yourself getting further and further into debt. If this is the case, then it is important that you address the situation. You can do this by **REDUCING YOUR NON-ESSENTIAL SPENDING** and/or **INCREASING YOUR INCOME.**

Track Your Daily Spending

circle the day →

| M T W Th F S Su | 1st |
Description	Amount
Daily Total:	

| M T W Th F S Su | 2nd |
Description	Amount
Daily Total:	

| M T W Th F S Su | 3rd |
Description	Amount
Daily Total:	

| M T W Th F S Su | 4th |
Description	Amount
Daily Total:	

M T W Th F S Su   **5**th

Description	Amount
Daily Total:	

M T W Th F S Su   **6**th

Description	Amount
Daily Total:	

M T W Th F S Su   **7**th

Description	Amount
Daily Total:	

M T W Th F S Su   **8**th

Description	Amount
Daily Total:	

So far this month, I have spent: **$**

Track Your Daily Spending

circle the day

M T W Th F S Su **9**th

Description	Amount

Daily Total:

M T W Th F S Su **10**th

Description	Amount

Daily Total:

M T W Th F S Su **11**th

Description	Amount

Daily Total:

M T W Th F S Su **12**th

Description	Amount

Daily Total:

M T W Th F S Su 13th

Description	Amount
Daily Total:	

M T W Th F S Su 14th

Description	Amount
Daily Total:	

M T W Th F S Su 15th

Description	Amount
Daily Total:	

M T W Th F S Su 16th

Description	Amount
Daily Total:	

So far this month, I have spent:

Track Your Daily Spending

circle the day

M T W Th F S Su **17**th

Description	Amount

Daily Total:

M T W Th F S Su **18**th

Description	Amount

Daily Total:

M T W Th F S Su **19**th

Description	Amount

Daily Total:

M T W Th F S Su **20**th

Description	Amount

Daily Total:

M T W Th F S Su **21**st

Description	Amount
Daily Total:	

M T W Th F S Su **22**nd

Description	Amount
Daily Total:	

M T W Th F S Su **23**rd

Description	Amount
Daily Total:	

M T W Th F S Su **24**th

Description	Amount
Daily Total:	

So far this month, I have spent: **$**

DEC

Track Your Daily Spending

circle the day

M T W Th F S Su 25th

Description	Amount

Daily Total:

M T W Th F S Su 26th

Description	Amount

Daily Total:

M T W Th F S Su 27th

Description	Amount

Daily Total:

M T W Th F S Su 28

Description	Amount

Daily Total:

M T W Th F S Su 29th

Description	Amount

Daily Total:

M T W Th F S Su 30th

Description	Amount

Daily Total:

M T W Th F S Su 31st

Description	Amount

Daily Total:

**** MONTHLY BUDGET CHECK ****

MONTHLY INCOME $

- TOTAL SPEND $ _____

        $ _____

How do you feel about your spending this month?

☹ 🙁 😐 🙂 😄

☐ ☐ ☐ ☐ ☐

I overspent   I was sensible!

What have you learned by tracking your spending this month? Write down your thoughts over the page.

WRITE DOWN YOUR THOUGHTS ABOUT THIS MONTH'S SPENDING

For example, you could ask yourself: Am I living within my means? Am I happier with my spending this month compared to last month? How can I cut down on non-essential spending? How can I increase my income? Can I afford a few treats? What lessons have I learned this month that I can put into practice next month?

Made in the USA
Las Vegas, NV
16 September 2021